Jack Ma: The Art of Dreaming & Succeeding Extraordinarily

—————— ✺✺✺✺ ——————

Jamie Morris

TABLE OF CONTENTS

INTRODUCTION 1

CHAPTER 1:   DREAM BIG 5

LESSON 1: BE A DREAMER 5

LESSON 2: BE A BELIEVER 12

LESSON 3: BE A VISIONARY 17

CHAPTER 2:   FIND YOUR GRIT 23

LESSON 4: BE TENACIOUS 23

LESSON 5: BE COURAGEOUS 30

LESSON 6: BE PATIENT 35

CHAPTER 3:   WEAR DIFFERENT
HATS 41

LESSON 7: BE A LEARNER 41

LESSON 8: BE A DOER 47

LESSON 9: BE AN INNOVATOR 52

CHAPTER 4: BUILD A WINNING TEAM **57**

LESSON 10: BE A LEADER.............. 57

LESSON 11: BE A FRIEND.............. 64

LESSON 12: BE WILLING TO ASK FOR HELP............................... 70

CHAPTER 5: REMEMBER THAT "H" MATTERS **77**

LESSON 13: BE HONEST................ 77

LESSON 14: BE HUMBLE............... 84

LESSON 15: BE HUMAN................. 90

CHAPTER 6: ENJOY THE RIDE...... **97**

LESSON 16: BE BOTH INSPIRED AND INSPIRING 97

LESSON 17: BE THE FUN............. 103

LESSON 18: BE A LITTLE CRAZY .. 110

CONCLUSION **115**

INTRODUCTION

To date, a search of self-help books on success in Amazon.com will deliver 44,019 results. Imagine that. There definitely is no dearth of literature on success in the market today, and rightly so, because a majority, if not all of us, have a desire to improve our lot in life. Many are yearning learn how to do so.

While people may subscribe to different definitions of success, I believe we will all agree that the steps to achieving and winning in life can be learned. One proven way to learn how to succeed is to follow those who walk the talk.

One such admirable role model is Mr. Jack Ma. Born in 1964 in Hangzhou as Ma Yun to storyteller and musician parents, Jack Ma has never been ashamed of his humble roots. Ma recalls that his family never had a lot of money while he and his siblings were growing up. He had enjoyed his childhood nonetheless by enjoying simple pleasures such as collecting and playing with crickets.

Even as a young boy, Jack already believed in the importance of education and hard work. In 1972, former US President Richard Nixon's visit in Hangzhou put the city on the map, driving more tourists to visit. Jack would make an hour's bike ride to the city's hotel to meet tourists. Over the next nine years, he would barter English lessons for tours around Hangzhou, gaining him fluency of the language. This love affair with English eventually sparked his passion to teach, which he did for several years even with little pay.

The course of Jack Ma's life has been marked with a lot of struggles. He faced several setbacks in getting himself to college, and even more in finding a job.

While his journey of bringing China closer to the rest of the world through the internet started with the amusing story of searching for the word "beer" online, his years of work were fraught with problems. Throughout all of these, he held on staunchly to his dreams of a better future not just for his family, but for his country.

Today, Jack Ma, with an estimated net worth of $37 billion, is China's richest billionaire, and the 7th richest tech tycoon in the world. E-Commerce giant Alibaba's IPO in 2014 has also been the New York Stock Exchange's largest offering.

While Ma's rags-to-riches may sound incredible to many, it is perhaps his underdog story that gives a lot of people hope – the hope that success is also within our reach. With careful analysis, one can see that while Jack had inspired a game-changing internet revolution in China, the principles he followed are not necessarily novel or untested.

Jack Ma: The Art of Dreaming &
Succeeding Extraordinarily

This book aims to show you time-proven
lessons in success, how these have been
applied in Jack's life, and more
importantly, how they can be applied
in yours. Each chapter discusses a
golden, and actionable nugget of wisdom
gleaned from his experiences in the
hopes of showing you that you too can
be a Jack Ma in your own life, by learning
how to dream extraordinarily and turn
these into reality.

CHAPTER 1:

DREAM BIG

LESSON 1: BE A DREAMER

**"Stay hungry and follow your dreams."
– Jack Ma**

Famous author, Brian Tracy, has made an astute observation about the world's most successful and influential persons. He says, "All successful men and women are big dreamers. They imagine what their future could be, ideal in every respect, and then they work every day toward their distant vision, that goal or purpose."

From Christopher Columbus to Steve Jobs, dreaming big has proven to be an important keystone to success. Jack Ma himself claimed this to be true, as he spoke in the 2014 Clinton Global Initiative Summit and said "We [have] success today because we had a dream 15 years ago. Fifteen years ago we believed the Internet could house small business."

The seeds of the Alibaba Group were born out of a literal and figurative detour Jack had made in 1995 during his first visit to the US. The year before that, he had just started his first business hinged on his English skills, the Haibo Translation Agency. The trip to United States was to actually help one of his clients collect payment from an American partner. As his meeting with the American turned out to be dangerously disastrous, he fled to Seattle to meet another friend.

It was there when his friend introduced him to computers and the Internet. Interestingly, Jack's first online search was for beer, which he later narrowed down to beer in China. After finding no information on China online, he and his friend created the first, albeit crude, webpage for the country. In a matter of hours, Jack started receiving a few emails, even if it was his first time to hear about email! This piqued his curiosity further, and led him to form China Pages, his first shot at an internet business.

As you will see in all the stories and biographies on Jack Ma, he had always gone after his dream, whether big or small. After developing China Pages, he took another shot four years later, by launching Alibaba.com with 17 of his friends in his apartment. His dreams kept on moving forward and getting bigger. At the start of the business, he inspired his partners into buying into the idea of an Alibaba IPO in 2002. And while this didn't come into fruition a little after a decade later, they still did it with a bang, with a $150 billion IPO.

Jack Ma: The Art of Dreaming & Succeeding Extraordinarily

Jack Ma emphatically says, "A lot of young people today don't have a dream today. Everyone should have a dream." Why is going after your dreams important? While some may find the idea to be overrated, actively seeking your aspirations matters even for the seemingly simple reason of nourishing your soul. Author Mark Manson says, "Meaning is the new luxury." Life in itself is hard. What makes it worthwhile is the meaning you ascribe to your journey. Without dreams for one's self or one's loved ones to reach for, daily living would be reduced to rote existence.

We are all given the innate capability to dream. In fact, dreaming comes naturally, especially to children. It is not surprising to hear little boys talking about wanting to be astronauts walking on the moon, or see little girls curtsy while they imagine themselves to be future queens. More often than not, clarity of dreams is seen in these small children. Unfortunately, as they grow older, they hear "No" all too often. "You can't do that! That's impossible!" As people age, we slowly become afraid of dreaming.

It is important for all of us to re-learn how to nurture our dreams. Rather than setting these aside, we need to connect with and follow these aspirations. We are the creators of our own dreams. As such, there is really no need to put a ceiling as to what we want to achieve.

After identifying your dream, what's important is that you make the first step towards it. Certainly, there is wisdom in Lao Tzu's saying, "A journey of a thousand miles begins with a single step." Jack Ma and Alibaba are examples that regardless of background or stature, you can move towards your goals. Ma shows us that:

- **There is no need to get other people's permission to get started.** – With its conservative environment and strict government bureaucracy, China was certainly not ripe to accept the idea of Internet-based businesses. However, this did not keep Ma from pitching his ideas not just to his family, but to the government as well.

- **There is no need to wait for the perfect set of circumstances.** – Previously a school teacher, Ma did not necessarily have the resources or the acumen to start his Internet venture. But he did so just the same, even if he had to borrow funds and operate from his own apartment!

- **There is no need to wait for your skills to be good.** -- Clearly, Jack Ma was no tech expert. But that didn't stop him from starting an E-Commerce business. Whatever he needed to learn about technology, he learned along the way. He likewise sought the help of experts who knew better than him.

Hearing Jack Ma's story, with all the obstacles he had to face, you will realize that you are the only one keeping yourself from taking the first step in moving towards your dreams. Go ahead and get started today!

"No matter how tough the chase is, you should always have the dream you saw on the first day. It'll keep you motivated and rescue you (from any weak thoughts)." – Jack Ma

LESSON 2: BE A BELIEVER

"Believe what you are doing. Whether people like it or people don't like it. Life is like a box of chocolate, you never know what you can get." – Jack Ma

Believe it or not, Jack Ma's personal hero is no other than the famous movie character played by Tom Hanks, Forrest Gump. If you will recall, just like Ma, Forrest Gump also came from humble beginnings. Even if faced various odds, Forrest had an amazing penchant for optimism as he followed his desires, whether it was playing ping-pong, catching shrimp or pursuing the love of his life, Jenny. He kept on putting one foot in front of the other, eventually running cross-country. Similarly, Jack's optimism has kept him plodding on in his journey in spite of various setbacks. Both men fiercely believe in their dreams, and they have never let obstacles get in the way of them.

CHAPTER 1: DREAM BIG

Why is it important to believe?

It's because doubt often leads to the death of your dream. It is not enough to have a spark of desire in your heart. It is equally important to fan the flames with a firm affirmation, to stoke them with reasons to believe. As the great Muhammad Ali has said, "It's the repetition of affirmation that leads to belief. And once that belief becomes a deep conviction, things begin to happen." Ma himself says, "Every entrepreneur must have faith, because only with faith will you not be tempted into doing this and that [instead of focusing]."

Jack Ma's belief encompasses many things and people. Firstly, he believed in himself and in his dreams. While others may have scoffed and laughed at his ideas, he hung on to them believing that he could make them happen. Jack likewise believed in the power of his team. He is popularly quoted to have said, "If we are a good team and know what we want to do, one of us can defeat ten of them."

Jack Ma: The Art of Dreaming & Succeeding Extraordinarily

Aside from believing in himself and the people around him, his belief was also grounded on a set of larger values. He is a staunch believer of his country and countrymen. His strong sense of nationalism has influenced his vision for his business. For him, "Alibaba is not just a job. It is a dream. It is a cause." Jack Ma believed in the power of small businesses and how helping them would unleash the country's economy. His vision is to create millions of job opportunities in China to lift millions as well out of poverty. As Jack beautifully says, "As a business person, I want the world to share the prosperity together."

Ma also underscores the importance of being bigger than yourself and of giving back. He is the epitome how one can use his talents in being generous. His early professional years as an educator were clearly a way of sharing his passions – English and teaching. He likewise believes in the power of investing in youth through mentoring. In an interview in South Korea's KBS in 2015, he spoke about learning and following a good model in your 20s and 30s and in practicing skill and excellence in your 40s and 50s. He says however that as one grows older, it is important to "work for the young people". In an article written for the Harvard Business Review in 2011, he articulated that it was key for his team at Alibaba to help inculcate good values in their junior staff.

Apart from the youth, Jack Ma also believes in the power of working with women. More than a third of the visionary founders of Alibaba in 1999 are women. As a percentage of employee population in the company, their numbers have increased from 34% in 2015 to almost 50% in 2017, which is definitely more than what can be said in their tech counterparts in Silicon Valley. In his keynote speech in Alibaba's Gateway '17 in Detroit, he referred to women as the of Alibaba's success, and in how women would all the more be very powerful in the 21st century.

Jack Ma's beliefs also extend to his concern for the environment, making him one of the world's greenest billionaires. Beyond public relations, Ma's environmental conscience is rooted in the recognition that wealth gives one greater responsibility over his environs and society in general. One shining example of his personal belief is how he decided to forego eating shark fin's soup once he discovered how it literally was destroying our oceans' shark population. In 2009, he also took on the role as Chairman of the Board of the Nature Conservancy's China program to actively find creative solutions to help the country's environmental issues.

Clearly, for Jack Ma, firm belief meant completely translating ideas into words, and later, into actions.

"If you have a different mindset, you will have a different outcome." – Jack Ma

LESSON 3: BE A VISIONARY

"I want to change history, do something important in my life, and influence individuals like we have with millions of small businesses on Alibaba." – Jack Ma

What's in name?

Why Alibaba? This is a curious question that has been asked by many as to why the business was named as such. The story goes with Jack being in a San Francisco coffee shop when he supposedly thought of the name. When he asked the waitress if she understood what "Alibaba" meant and she answered favorably, he decided it was the perfect name! Jack Ma's apt choice in itself clearly reflects how he was already a masterful visionary even at the onset of his business. It was clear to him early on that his startup E-Commerce business in China would eventually be a global one. He therefore selected

"Alibaba" because it was easily pronounced and well-recognized. Appropriately, it also meant "open sesame" which for him meant opening gateways for small entrepreneurs, and opening China to reach out to the rest of the world. And that's just naming his company! A big thinker, right?

The Alibaba Group's official website articulates conglomerate's mission to "make it easy to do business anywhere". While it may seem to be a simple statement, it also reflects how Jack Ma and his team's intent to continue reshaping retail and transforming the market immeasurably.

What began as a humble start-up in an apartment 18 years ago, has now grown as one of the world's biggest E-Commerce giants. From a single company, Alibaba has formed a complete digital ecosystem where consumers can interact and liaise with brands, merchants and the company's strategic partners. Alibaba.com, the group's first business is a global trading marketplace for agents, manufacturers, exporters and retailers. Similarly, 1688.com is an online marketplace connecting buyers and sellers in China. It also serves as a wholesale channel for vendors selling through Alibaba's retail avenues. Taobao Marketplace is Alibaba's social platform for retail shopping, with its customers' experiences personalized through big data analytics. While also dedicated to retail shoppers, Tmall on the other hand, carries internationally branded and more premium items. AliExpress' business meanwhile is dedicated to serving retail clientele globally, with most of the buyers coming from the United States and Europe. Ant Financial Services Group provides technology for the clients' digital payments, as well as financing for the merchants partnered with the core businesses. The Alibaba Group's interests also lie in marketing technology, through Alimama.com, cloud computing and services through Alibaba Cloud, and logistics data through Cainiao Network. Interestingly, Jack Ma and his team's vision has been able to create a singular and convenient channel where the wholesale and retail markets can conduct all their buying, selling, payment and financing activities.

Why is vision important? Everything starts with a vision. Your vision gives you something to aspire for and guides you. A common vision brings a leader and his team to work towards the same goals. People generally want to follow a leader who knows where he is going. This is exactly why Jack's 17 friends agree to join him in 1999 – they saw, and more importantly, bought in to his vision.

Even at that time, Jack understood where he wanted to go. His speech to his friends said it all. "I've always said our competitors are not domestic websites but overseas websites. Our competitors are not in China but in Silicon Valley. So first, we should position Alibaba as a global website not just a domestic website." And that is exactly where they took a step towards.

While some of us may already have a clear vision of what they want in their life and business even at an early age, there are others who have difficulty identifying theirs. If this is your case, there is no need to fret.

How do you develop your vision? It all starts with asking questions. What do you want? Who do you want to become? Once you start forming answers to these, it will help to then ask yourself, "Why?" so as to understand your reasons behind these.

The next step is to develop clarity in your vision and to work out articulating even its smallest detail. While this may take time, it is an important exercise to allow you to focus on what's really essential to your vision. Gary Keller, author of "The One Thing", recommends asking the Focusing Question, "What's the ONE Thing you can do such that by doing it everything else will be easier or unnecessary?" Clarity allows you to then plan for the smaller steps you need to take to get to your goal. Keller recommends creating an environment wherein you can create a domino effect for your vision, where each domino is sequentially toppled until the last is reached. In the same way, the journey to what it is you really aspire for happens step by step as you achieve your smaller goals. After that, it becomes all about moving forward daily.

"The quality of a good leader therefore is his vision, tenacity, and his capability." – Jack Ma

CHAPTER 2:

FIND YOUR GRIT

LESSON 4: BE TENACIOUS

"If you don't give up, you still have a chance. Giving up is the greatest failure." – Jack Ma

"I am not concerned that you have fallen — I am concerned that you arise." The wisdom in these words by Abraham Lincoln certainly ring true in Jack Ma's life. Perhaps, if we were to identify a single defining trait of Ma in his journey to success, it would be his tenacity.

In multiple interviews and speeches, Jack often spoke of the numerous times he had faced rejection growing up. "I failed a key primary school test 2 times, I failed the middle school test 3 times, I failed the college entrance exam 2 times and when I graduated, I was rejected for most jobs I applied for out of college." He jokingly talks about his desire to teach in Harvard because his application had been turned down ten times.

It was the same tune for his early working years, as he was rejected from 30 jobs! A famous anecdote narrates how he was the only one out of 24 manager applicants to KFC in China and the only one out of 5 police officers to be rejected. He was even told, "You're no good."

While others would find this funny post-mortem, it certainly could not have been a pleasant experience for Jack at that time. This, however, did not prevent him from pushing on.

Jack Ma likewise ran across many walls in his dream of bringing E-Commerce to China. His first venture, China Pages, was one of the country's first formally registered internet companies. He looked for various local businesses to advertise in his website. In his documentary "Crocodile in the Yangtze", Portis Erisman, who worked with Ma in Alibaba for nine years, showed how Ma made multiple visits to government offices in Beijing to solicit their support. He patiently explained to them how people from other countries were now able to do business with other Asian countries like Singapore, Taiwan and Hong Kong using their computers, and how this wasn't possible with China, because of the lack of the country's presence online. These officials however repeatedly rejected his ideas and expressed their hesitation in extending support, especially since at that time media and information dissemination were sensitive areas politically. Jack also developed another website to for China's Olympic bid, but this too did not get government's support.

Realizing that it was perhaps too early for China to appreciate the Internet, Ma decided to let go of his goal, at least for the time being. He however did not lose his interest for the Internet and E-Commerce completely. He started working with the country's Ministry of Foreign Trade and Economic Cooperation to continue help building websites. In 1999, he got on the saddle once more, now with his friends, to start Alibaba.com, his own China-based business-to-business marketplace.

Even though the team was overflowing with excitement, this did not necessarily mean that everything was smooth sailing from thereon. They first had to face challenges in getting funding. In fact, due to limited resources, their initial operations were limited to Jack's apartment! Ma initially tried to raise support from Silicon Valley, but he was met with the criticism that his business model appeared to be unsustainable. Eventually, Alibaba found partners with Goldman Sachs and Softbank which invested with them five million dollars and twenty million dollars respectively.

CHAPTER 2: FIND YOUR GRIT

Soon after, Alibaba launched itself to the media, and things seemed to ride on a positive note, with the internet boom having reached China. Although Alibaba was still not making revenues, Ma made a bold move to transfer operations to the US. The quick expansion of the organization and the move to America did not turn out well for the company, and Jack had to reverse his decision ultimately.

In 2001, Alibaba's finally started to pay off. They struck gold with the discovery that there were companies willing pay a premium to go up in the search page rankings. Leveraging on this new insight, Alibaba found itself no longer in the red, and with 500,000 yuan in profit to boot.

Psychologist Angela Duckworth describes grit or tenacity as a combination of resilience in adversity and the ability to focus long-term on a passion or a goal. She further defines this as "having stamina" and "sticking with your future, day in and day out." If anything at all,

Jack Ma: The Art of Dreaming &
Succeeding Extraordinarily

Jack Ma is the picture of grit. In spite of
seemingly insurmountable challenges,
Ma never gave up. He believed that "If
you don't go through a storm, you will
never see a rainbow." Jack
understood that achieving success also
meant having resilience to endure the
necessary sacrifices.

How can you learn resilience? While
many things can be learned vicariously
through reading and education, tenacity
is really developed by facing difficulties
head on. Ma himself states, "Once you
have been through hardships, grievances
and disappointments, only then will you
understand what is resilience."

It is important to note though, that grit
does not mean stubbornly repeating the
same mistakes. As the famous quote
goes, "Insanity is doing the same thing
over and over again and expecting
different results." While tenacity means
always keeping your eye on the goal, and
getting back up again after falling, it also
means being willing to find the right

strategies to hit your target. It likewise means understanding that certain goals also require proper timing. Such is the case when Ma took a break from pitching to the government in 1995.

Jack Ma's journey to success is an inspiring one because he had an ordinary background, just like the majority of us. His story dispels the myth that success strictly requires talent. Finally, he is proof that learning grit is a choice, and that we can all choose to be gritty.

"No matter what your current condition, how or where you grew up, or what education or training you feel you lack, you can be successful in your chosen endeavor. It is spirit, fortitude, and hardiness that matter more than where you start." – Jack Ma

LESSON 5: BE COURAGEOUS

"You will never learn to swim until you are in the water." – Jack Ma

Merriam-Webster defines courage as "mental or moral strength to venture, persevere, and withstand danger, fear, or difficulty." Courage is what distinguishes true leaders from good managers, and what spells the difference between businesses that change industries and ones that merely stay afloat.

Even as young, scrawny child, Jack Ma already had the makings of a brave man. He had used to get into fights with his classmates, but he was never afraid of his opponents, even if they were actually bigger than him. Growing up, with Hangzhou becoming a tourist mecca, he was gutsy enough to befriend the foreigners so that he could learn English from them. In fact, he actually got the nickname "Jack" from the friends he made.

CHAPTER 2: FIND YOUR GRIT

In business, courage is the ability to take big, calculated risks in order to grow or innovate. Even early on in business, Jack took bold leaps in speaking with the government and investors to pitch his ideas. His courage has always been seen in his daring moves, such as the bid to launch Alibaba to the media, or to transfer operations to the United States.

A leader's courage is often what inspires his team, especially during trying times. Jack's courage rallied his Alibaba team countless times in their journey, like the dry spell when they were not yet making money, or when they had to take operations to their own homes when SARs hit China.

At the heart of it, courage must be rooted in a strong vision and an unwavering belief in one's dreams. It will be difficult for anyone to be strong if their "why" is not clear. In Jack's case, his hopes for both Alibaba and China, fueled his courage even if naysayers had so many doubts.

Jack Ma: The Art of Dreaming &
Succeeding Extraordinarily

Courage must also be anchored on humility and the willingness to learn. Albert Einstein once said, "A person who never made any mistake never tried anything new." Jack Ma has been quoted to have humbly said that Alibaba was "1,001 mistakes." However, he also believes that mistakes should be welcomed as "wonderful revenue" for what can be learned from them.

As many have often quoted, courage does not really mean the absence of fear. It is moving forward in spite of it. In his documentary, Portis Erisman spoke of the time when Jack reversed his decision to move to the US and they had to shut down operations. This was supposedly his first time to have felt Jack's resolve seem to waver. Like all of us, Ma is also human, with his own vulnerabilities and fears. What sets him apart though, like many outstanding leaders and achievers, is his ability find his light, even in the midst of all this darkness.

Can courage be taught? While some may say it is difficult to do so, just like all other habits, courage can be practiced. Here are a few suggestions:

- **Find Role Models** – A role model is an affirmation and a reminder that indeed something you aspire for can be achieved. Find a role model of courage that you can relate to and follow.

- **Try Something New** – While seemingly insignificant, it takes courage to try something different. This will be good practice for finding the will to do bigger things.

- **Say What You Feel** – More often than not, we hold back on expressing our thoughts and emotions for fear that these will not be received well. Without losing tact of course, practice being more candid in sharing your opinions to your friends and colleagues.

"We're never in lack of money. We lack people with dreams, (people) who can die for those dreams." – Jack Ma

LESSON 6: BE PATIENT

"The very important thing you should have is patience." – Jack Ma

Jack Ma's interests outside his business dealings show a lot about him as a person. In his free time, he practices Tai Chi not just as a form of exercise, but also its philosophy. Ma believes in Tai Chi so much that he has formed the Taiji Zen Online Academy with renowned actor Jet Li and he teaches courses to fellow entrepreneurs. A follower since 1988, Ma had also consciously hired Tai Chi master Li Tianjin as his personal bodyguard, instead of the more conventional, muscled choices.

What is Tai Chi? Tai chi is a non-defensive form of martial arts and an exercise that embraces one's mind, body and spirit. Those who don't practice the art often associate it with elderly folk exercising early morning in parks. However, beyond being a pastime, Tai Chi teaches value-laden principles of remaining calm, following the flow of one's strengths, and abandoning one's burdens. Jack believes in the importance of keeping calm, so that "you will find a way out." Tai Chi is likewise teaches patience, since one has to deliberately practice slow movements and movement against gentle resistance. Newcomers to the art, especially those that lead high-paced, frenetic schedules, often find it difficult to slow down. Regular patient practice however will show them that the slow, deliberate actions, much like the gentle flow of water in a river, can create much inner strength.

What is the value of practicing patience? Patience is a valuable resource when it comes to decision- making, especially in business. While speed is critical in gaining a share of the market, patience and mindfulness are likewise important in keeping entrepreneurs grounded in the present and attuned to the market. This allows leaders to appreciate both the trees and the forest, helping make for smarter choices for their business. Patience also teaches a person self-control. Mastery over one's emotions is key in making rational and logical plans. As businesses grow, these become all the more important as bigger teams and resources require more strategic deployment.

Some shun the idea of patience with the mistaken idea that it means just passively waiting. It is in fact, quite the opposite, as evidenced by Jack Ma's life. Patience is inextricably related to grit and resilience. It means keeping the faith, even when the surrounding climate encourages you to quit. It means continuing doing what you believe in, even if the results don't show quickly. Patience is doing the right things, even when they're not fun to do. It means understanding that progress is infinitely more important than perfection.

Alibaba's journey to business success is a wonderful example of patience. Jack Ma and his team had enough perseverance in developing in their business model even if it was not immediately profitable. It took them many iterations to find what worked with the businesses that advertised with them, but when they finally did, it brought in the revenues like a gold mine.

For start-ups, patience is likewise important in finding and developing in partners. Trust is always built over time. Venture capitalists, especially those have built their wealth the hard way, won't invest in any new business with the snap of a finger, and not without doing proper due diligence. The same was clearly seen Alibaba. It took Jack the support of different team members and multiple trips to get their investors on board.

With the ever growing pressure of high-yielding performance in the workplace, business leaders are also encouraged to practice patience in dealing with their employees. They will find that now more than ever, their teams look to them to practice open-mindedness and compassion in their leadership. A lack of these can mean that their employees will find it all too easy to jump ship, even to their competitors.

Patience indeed is a virtue. What's good though, is that like most of the other things in life, it can be learned. Elon Musk himself has been quoted to have said, "Patience is a virtue, and I'm learning patience."

How do you grow your patience? One way is to start with yourself, by deliberately taking a break to slow down. A frenetic pace at work over the long haul will tend to wear you down, whereas practicing mindfulness can recharge you. Patience with other people can also be learned by trying to see the world from their lens. This can give you a glimpse of other perspectives. Patience likewise can be developed by learning how to practice active and emphatic listening. While this may take time, it is only listening that we can understand our team's journey better.

Another tried and tested method, is to do as Jack did. Why not try learning Tai Chi for yourself perhaps?

"You've got to have patience to make money here." – Jack Ma

CHAPTER 3:

WEAR DIFFERENT HATS

LESSON 7: BE A LEARNER

"A stupid thing – if you improve it every day, it is going to be very smart." – Jack Ma

Jack Ma is living proof that your circumstances need not restrict you from achieving success in life. His humble background did not automatically give him access to resources that one born with a silver spoon would more easily have. Most of the anecdotes about Ma tell about how started learning English by himself at the young age of 12. And he worked for this the hard way, by biking 40 minutes every morning to act as a tour guide to foreigners in exchange for English lessons. One can only imagine how difficult this could have been, especially at a time and in an environment like China's where only a minority were fluent in English. Later on, he even had to face a lot of rejection in applying for schools. While for some, facing such difficulties would compel them to quit, this did not quell his desire to improve himself.

Although Jack took many pains to get himself educated, he does not necessarily believe that formal education is the sole key to success. In fact, he has supposedly advised his soon that he need not be at the top of his academics. He says that in principle, it is ok to be an average student, and use his free time

to learn other skills, rather than solely focusing on grades alone. Jack espouses instilling in one's self an entrepreneurial spirit that constantly seeks learning and growth.

CHAPTER 3: WEAR DIFFERENT HATS

How can you become a lifelong learner? You can commit to a few simple steps daily to do so. One way is to choose to read a book fifteen minutes each day. If we assume to fifteen minutes to be equivalent to fifteen pages, it would mean a good 450 pages each month. That would be equivalent to a book or two. Imagine the power in having read at least 12 new books in a year.

How do you schedule your 15-minute read daily? Again, this is a matter of choice as well. To make it easier, you can choose to break this up in smaller chunks, say 5-minute periods. You can then read a section for 5 minutes when you wake up, another section after lunch, and another prior to going to bed. All of us will spend a few minutes here and there anyway doing things which don't necessarily add value. You might as well make the time count.

Another way is to listen regularly to personal development audio books. While this may sound like a tall order, you can also carve out time for this, by plugging in to the material during your daily commute, or while doing household chores. If you are so inclined, you can splurge a bit on monthly subscription to programs like Audible, but you can also find websites where audio books are shared for free. You can also watch or listen to videos on a variety of topics from influential speakers from websites like TED.com. This way, you can gain different perspectives or learn about other fields.

Of course, a different kind of learning can be gained "on the job". To supplement your learning from educational materials, you can likewise help yourself grow by finding a mentor you can consult or shadow with. It can be as simple as seeking out this person and getting their buy-in for a regular coaching session. Alternately, it can be more structured with the use of platforms like Grow360.com where you can document your personal development program and track your progress.

CHAPTER 3: WEAR DIFFERENT HATS

Aside from expanding skillsets, Jack also believes greatly in learning from rejection and failures. According to Jack, he took his multiple employment rejections as God's cue that he should probably consider working for himself instead of forcing himself to get a job. He likewise sees failure as a catalyst that to be used to drive innovation. He says, "You have to get used to failure. If you can't, then how you win?" Again, this resilient perspective on failure and rejection is inextricably related to how he practices grit. Only with a rooted sense of determination can a person like Jack Ma find the positive in difficult situations.

How can you learn from failure then? Failure can serve as a great teacher, only if it is seen under the lens of introspection. After you allow yourself go to through failure's associated emotions, it will be best to review three things – your planning, your preparation and your execution. How sufficiently did you plan prior to your task? Did you map out possible challenges and corresponding workarounds? Did you prepare your backup plan? How well did you implement your plans? Were you consistent with your work ethic? These are a few guide questions that when answered honestly, can be a gold mine in analyzing what went well and what went wrong in your efforts.

Jack Ma's sincere belief that mistakes can be treated as revenues if we choose to learn from them is certainly worth practicing. As often says, "Instead of learning from other people's success, learn from their mistakes."

"Remember that your past successes may lead to your future failure. However, if you learn a lesson from every failure, then you may ultimately succeed." – Jack Ma

LESSON 8: BE A DOER

"Instead of your heart beats faster, why not you just act faster a bit; instead of just thinking about it, why not do something about it." – Jack Ma

Of course, all the learning in the world will not serve good use if these are left as theories. As the famous poet, Saadi of Shiraz, has said," However much you study, you cannot know without action. A donkey laden with books is neither an intellectual nor a wise man. Empty of essence, what learning has he whether upon him is firewood or book?" Also, with the rate that current technology is allowing us to access data, the glut of information available can quickly become irrelevant if hypothesis are not tried, tested or tweaked, thus the importance of taking action quickly. Acquiring knowledge and being analytical are no longer sufficient. Information can only take you so far. At a certain point, the business of doing has to start. Only with trial and error can we start finding workable solutions to our problems.

Aside from learning, Jack Ma is a firm believer of taking action. He says, "Make the move. Make the action. To everybody, to any person, tomorrow is new." He is not one to be averse to rolling out a new initiative. His first webpage is in fact the perfect example! If you'll recall his story of discovering the internet, he had his first website on China, albeit crude, up and running hours after his friend showed him all about the World Wide Web. While others would often wait for the perfect time to implement their plans, even with limited resources, Jack rolled up his sleeves and went to work. It did not matter if they had to build Alibaba from his apartment, or if they had to travel far and wide to find investors, or if their team had to hole up working from home during the SARS outbreak, they nonetheless got their jobs done. His work ethic is very much similar to renowned artist Vincent Van Gogh's. Van Gogh is famous for having created over 2,000 paintings in the span of a decade, because he laboriously worked on his art daily. He too believed in the power of getting started and re-committing daily to one's goals.

Ma is also understands the power of trying and taking chances. "If you've never tried, how will you ever know if there's any chance?" Vincent Van Gogh similarly espoused the need to go through the motions even though uncertain of whether the outcome would be good or bad. Not all of Jack's moves were always right. There were many times when his decisions, such as their bid for US operations, proved to be very costly. However, he still stands by his mantra of acting the soonest. In this day and age, he believes, "A wrong decision is better than no decision at the internet time." All too often, our anxieties, as well as the amount of information at hand, create "analysis paralysis" in us. We become overwhelmed with options which confound us. Since nobody likes to be wrong, we tend to stall making decisions for fear of making mistakes.

How can you overcome analysis paralysis in decision-making and turn yourself into a doer? First of all, it's important to determine the difference between big and small decisions. The scale of the decision has to be considered since more impactful items will likely require more thorough evaluation. Second, if it will require some planning, it is critical for you to give yourself a deadline as to when to make the move. Depending on the complexity of the matter, it will also help to bring in other relevant experts just so you can do a reality check and ground your decision. Once you've made peace with your decision, you would also need to curb your curiosity and refrain from second-guessing yourself. You then need to make peace with the fact that whatever you choose to do will never please everyone. Aside from this, it is important for you to buy into the belief that progress is more important than perfection. Waiting for the perfect choice or option to be determined can come at a much higher price of missed opportunities. While it is important to do due diligence, there is also merit in making gut decisions. In times like these, don't be afraid to be like Jack, and do Nike - just do it!

"I like to play cards. I'm not very good because I don't want to calculate. I just play by instinct. But I've learned a lot of business philosophy by playing poker." – Jack Ma

LESSON 9: BE AN INNOVATOR

"Opportunity lies in the place where complaints are." – Jack Ma

These days the word "innovator" has become a catchphrase used all too frequently. We often hear how businesses or leaders need to "drive innovation" or become "gamechangers". While all of these sound exciting, we often ask ourselves, "What does really mean?"

While we often associate innovation with creativity, innovative leadership is said to go beyond that. The CEO or the head of a team need not necessarily be the creative genius or the idea generator. The leader however must have a think-out-of-the-box attitude, and must be able to cultivate that culture in the organization. Innovative leadership means recognizing ideas with potential, communicating this vision within the team, and driving this all the way to implementation. For larger, complex-scale projects, this manner of leadership also finds ways to sustain the commitment to the goal, even over a long period of time.

Innovative leaders work with a powerful imagination. But they do not work alone. They work with other creative forces who can build on their ideas to make these grow. As such, you can say that innovative leadership also requires a good measure of humility and willingness to accept help from others.

The late Walt Disney once said, "Get a good idea and stay with it. Dog it, and work at it until it's done right." This is the very definition of innovativeness, and this is also what Jack Ma has been doing for the Alibaba Group over many years.

In itself, the seeds of Alibaba.com were already very novel in China at the time Jack and his team were conceptualizing it. While Chinese commerce carried a long history, the country solely operated on brick- and-mortar businesses. They also largely focused inward. So at that time, small businesses considering to take their products internationally was largely unheard of. Jack saw that the Internet could help connect businesses in remote areas in China which found travel for trade difficult and expensive. He also believed opening up China to the rest of the world for business was an excellent idea. More importantly, in his heart, he knew that this would be good for his fellowmen, so he pursued it relentlessly.

For Jack, excellent entrepreneurs are problem-solvers. He says that people face many problems daily, and good businesses are the ones who are able to find problems that they can solve and create niches for themselves. Jack and his team won the market with Alibaba and Taobao when they decided to delay profits by offering the services for free, allowing their users to do business worry-free. In a market where their stiffest competition remarked, "free is not a business model," their move certainly went against the grain. In the war between the Alibaba group and eBay, they were able to carve a niche for Taobao by designing it in such a way that users felt like they belonged to a community, making the platform very relatable. In itself, the Alibaba ecosystem is gamechanging as it offers wholesale trade, retail trade payments and financing in one self-supporting platform. And the fact that over 100 million people use Alibaba daily is more than enough to show that Ma's model is an excellent one.

He also says that innovation comes from looking at something from various perspectives. One way is to look at situation in a forward-looking manner. What can happen in the future? Another way is to evaluate an idea from an outsider's perspective. In the case of Chinese business, he always asks himself about the world's perspective.

Even after the success of Alibaba, Jack maintains the need to innovate. He even goes beyond this by espousing the need to pass on the attitude and culture to the youth. "We have to teach our kids to be very, very innovative, very creative," he said. "In this way, we can create jobs for our own kids." Again, this is rooted in his deep sense of nationalism. He selflessly believes in investing in the youth as a means of ensuring China's continued growth in the future.

Truly, Jack Ma's attitude on innovation leads the way, so much so that he has been ranked the 3rd

highest in the global tech innovation visionary survey by KPMG, only below Steve Jobs and Elon Musk.

**"Never ever compete on prices. Instead compete on services and innovation."
– Jack Ma**

CHAPTER 4:

BUILD A WINNING TEAM

LESSON 10: BE A LEADER

"If you want your life to be simple, you shouldn't be a leader." – Jack Ma

With the outstanding achievements of Alibaba, Jack Ma has been the subject of many leadership studies seeking to understand his leadership and management style, to see his formula for success. These studies have observed that Ma in fact has been quite flexible to use various management styles over the course of his leadership.

In Alibaba's early years, Ma and his core group managed in an autocratic and conductive manner, limiting decisions only between Ma and his key advisors. During this period, these styles were more suited since at the beginning, the organization needed to be focused on a singular guiding vision. The paternalistic system was also effective because the group was still small enough for Ma to know everyone on board at a personal level.

Jack Ma transitioned to using a persuasive management style when Alibaba tried to expand internationally. At this stage, he realized he had to bring in other experts to help, but at the same time, he had to convince his local partners and investors that this was needed. A persuasive management style is still similar to an autocratic style, however, in this style, the manager is more attuned to the needs of his team, and is able convince them of how they will benefit from a particular corporate decision.

CHAPTER 4: BUILD A WINNING TEAM

With the growth of Alibaba and its workforce, Ma has begun using a more democratic management style, as well as management by wandering around. In these styles, there is more two-way communication and feedback from employees. Decision-making is also more inclusive. Ma is seen to be keeping up with the times, especially since the Alibaba employee population is moving towards a younger workforce. Ma strongly believes that the country's and his company's future lie in the youth, thus Alibaba seeks to keep them engaged through channels such as Aliway and Ali Ten Groups.

Aside from being attuned to the organization's pulse, and being flexible enough to adapt to it, Jack Ma's leadership has been lauded because it has inspired loyalty from such a large base. What is even more fascinating is that Ma didn't fit the usual CEO profile. He wasn't tagged as a likely technopreneur especially since he had no formal tech background, which even he himself candidly admits.

Brian Tracy has aptly said, "Become the kind of leader that people would follow voluntarily; even if you had no title or position." While Jack Ma is not one of the usual suspects, he clearly has been deemed worthy of being followed.

Certainly, there are invaluable lessons that can be learned with how Jack Ma practices leadership. Here are a few worth taking home:

- **Leading with Words** – Ma believes that the success of any business was hinged on trust, and that trust could only be built with honesty. In doing business with clients, Ma and his team were upfront with them about the fact that while E-Commerce was positioned to have a great future, the results at that time would come in slow. Alibaba employees are likewise trained to never accept any form of bribery. This has helped the company earn the belief and trust of the market.

- **Leading by Example** – According to Simon Sinek, "Leaders go first and open a path." Rather than just delegating the gritty work to his team, Ma himself dives in head on and takes a hands-on approach with work. During Alibaba's start-up years, he would travel to even as far as Silicon Valley to pitch his business model.

- **Leading from the Heart** – Ma himself has said that he doesn't want to run a business just to make money. Ma is well-loved because he exudes warmth and care for the people around him. Alibaba's large spending for activities geared towards employee recreation is solid proof of this. Jack Ma is followed because his team recognizes his intentions of bringing people along with him to succeed. There are even stories of how Ma used to give equity to the high school students who helped him when Alibaba was just starting out.

- **Leading through Service** – In 1970, Robert Greenleaf coined the term "servant leadership" by saying "The servant-leader is servant first... It begins with the natural feeling that one wants to serve, to serve first." Jack Ma's mission is to use Alibaba as an enabler for E-Commerce to thrive, not just for profit, but for service. In his words, "Going public three years ago reinforced our sense of mission, that while public shareholders expect us to be profitable, our raison d'être cannot be merely to make money....As one of the world's largest technology companies with a mission focused on serving small business, we must contribute to the sustainable development of a healthy world economy... We aim to be a platform that will enable the creation of 100 million jobs, serve two billion consumers and support 10 million profitable small businesses." Grounded in his own humble background, Ma is now seeking to help others find their own success. Ma and his team are now working with Chinese villages with no internet to help them build the required infrastructure. The team then provides a few computers to locals with enough tech savvy to allow them to take orders for the rest of the village. Successful models include Huang Jianqiao, previously a farmer but now turned online bag store owner, who now does business of $4.8 million dollars yearly because of this platform.

"In Taoism, the best leadership is not leading at all." – Jack Ma

LESSON 11: BE A FRIEND

"Friendship is far too valuable to be measured." – Jack Ma

Early in 2017, Jack Ma made a very generous donation of twenty million dollars (or AU\$26.4 million) to the University of Newcastle. The large sum was the first and largest donation of its kind given to the university. This was likewise the first donation of the Jack Ma Foundation to the country. The pledge was made to honor Jack Ma's special friendship with the Morley family.

Jack first met patriarch Ken Morley and his family in Hangzhou in in 1980, while they were on a tour with the Australia-China Friendship Society. Ken's son, David, was also a teenager as the same age as Jack and he started helping Ma practice his English. In 1985, Jack visited the Morley family in Australia, taking his first overseas trip to spend a one-month vacation with them. This trip opened up his perspective about many things. While he initially perceived China to be the "richest, happiest country in the world", he learned to think more critically after seeing another part of the world. Jack recalls, "The culture, the landscape and most importantly its people had a profound positive impact on my view of the world at that time." He credits the trip to be one of his most life-changing experiences and emphasizes how experiencing the world lets you learn differently from learning through academics.

In the years to follow, Jack would continue to be friends with the family, with Ken becoming a very influential person in his life. Ken made several more trips to China to help in the school where Jack taught. He also supported Jack's first apartment purchase.

So high was Jack's regard for the Morley family that Jack himself went to Newcastle personally to announce the scholarship program. The Ma & Morley

Scholarship Program aims to uplift indigenous scholars and financially challenged students. Initially, the scholarship will help 30 students. At full capacity however, the program, designed to reflect values of Ma and Morley's special friendship, is projected to support around 90 students. David Morley proudly says, "Dad would be extremely proud of Jack's commitment to making a difference to students in our hometown, and so touched that their close friendship has led to this program, which will transform the futures of hundreds of University of Newcastle students, to hopefully do good things in the world."The Ma & Morley Scholarship Program is a wonderful testament to how Jack believes in the power of friendship and gratitude.

Why is friendship important? It is a good to have a strong circle of friends outside your family for a variety of reasons. If you allow them to, friends can play a very important role in your life. As in the case of Jack Ma, the quality of people you surround yourself with can influence your attitudes and behavior. As Jim Rohn says, "You are the average of the five people you spend the most time with."

As pillars of their teams and organizations, people look to their leaders for strength and guidance. As such, leaders are often fraught with anxiety, especially with the great weight of responsibilities they carry. A strong support group from your circle of friends can help ease this burden. Opening up to trusted friends can help since they can provide a safe space for you to process your concerns.

Aside from cheering you on, friends can help ground you. They can provide various perspectives in how you can understand or face your challenges. Likewise, spending time with loved ones and friends outside work hours provides for better work-life balance. After all, it's also important to find time for relaxation in the midst of one's busy schedule.

Jack Ma: The Art of Dreaming & Succeeding Extraordinarily

Jack Ma cautions people in starting businesses with their close friends as downturns can affect the relationship. He does advise however to build close relationships with business partners and teammates. This is clearly seen in how he treats his team at Alibaba. Be it celebrations for the team's milestones, or his own candid performances and impersonations, Jack always finds ways to help build camaraderie in the group.

While it is important for a leader to never blur the lines between being a boss and being a friend, building friendships at work also pays off with a number of benefits. Aside from helping improve job satisfaction and productivity, studies show that co-workers who are personally invested in each other make for a stronger, more effective team. Teams like these are also more geared to deal with setbacks more resiliently. With its sustained success over the years, the Alibaba team is perfect example of how an organization strengthened by the ties of friendship is positioned to thrive.

"We used to take these great hikes on the Great Wall... From our hikes, we developed a friendship that ended up with us combining forces in forming this new Chinese company." – Jack Ma

LESSON 12: BE WILLING TO ASK FOR HELP

"You need the right people with you, not the best people." – Jack Ma

Among other things, Jack Ma is well-known for his nuggets of wisdom on a great deal of matters, including building one's team. In developing organizations, successful leaders like Jack Ma, Mark Zuckerberg and the late Steve Jobs believe in getting the right people on board their teams. Ma subscribes to hiring the right people for the job, not necessarily the best ones. As a teacher, he also recognizes that he may not know everything. In fact, he humbly admits that he is not an expert in accounting or marketing. Nor is he really a technology genius. As such, he believes in seeking help from the right people. His philosophy is to hire people who are smarter than him, and to eventually help them become more successful than him. Never greedy for power, he also smartly says, "If you think he will be your boss in five years, hire him."

Most people have the misconception a good leader, to project strength, should seek to overcome challenges by himself. Most of us are not programmed to ask for help. We find it to be a display of weakness or dependence. We find ourselves worried either about burdening other people, or about not being able to reciprocate help that's received. The perfectionists in us worry about losing control over the task at hand, or about not being able to do it fast enough if other people get involved. As such, we try to do everything by ourselves, thinking that our achievement would be greater in doing so. Unfortunately, rather than being helpful, this practice ends up holding a leader and his team back from becoming successful.

Why is it important to get the support of other people? Firstly, it allows us to be more efficient with our resources. Rather than squandering these with repeated ineffective efforts, we are able to focus more on our strengths when get experts with the appropriate skills on board. Also, we enable the rest of our team to shine. This nurtures their potential, and in turn helps grow their trust and loyalty. Asking for help shows a leader's humility and actually makes him or her more relatable with the group. Instead of it being a weakness, courageously asking for support makes leaders stronger.

As legendary coach John Wooden has said, "We're all imperfect and we all have needs. The weak usually do not ask for help, so they stay weak. If we recognize that we are imperfect, we will ask for help and we will pray for the guidance necessary to bring positive results to whatever we are doing." Smart and successful leaders have no qualms about asking for help. They know their organization and outside affiliates well enough to know who to ask help from. They know when to ask for help. Before enlisting others' assistance, they do the necessary due diligence, and they exhaust all options they are able to do on their own. They also know the best way to ask for help.

How can a leader make asking for help easier? First, it's important to have a clear vision of what you intend to achieve, and what's needed to get it done. Next, it's critical to clarify what assistance exactly is needed so that the necessary requests can be framed properly. Similar to goals, requests for help should also be phrased in a SMART manner. It is easier to respond positively to a request which is Specific, Meaningful, Action-oriented, Real, and Time-bound. This will allow the other party to decide if they are in a position to help. Of course, it's also important not to make any assumptions about the third party's willingness and capability to help. On top of all of these, excellent leaders develop a culture in their team that fosters humility and openness to ask for assistance.

Jack Ma: The Art of Dreaming & Succeeding Extraordinarily

Jack Ma built his success brick by brick, but he did not do this by himself. He was open to receiving help and many were willing to share it. Prior to launching Alibaba, he sat down with 24 friends to ask their opinion. And although they didn't really think that Jack's idea would work, he found it important to tinker with their input before he dismissed their comments. Aside from them, other friends helped along the way. The Morleys supported him financially during the period in his life that he was struggling financially. He sought Porter Erisman's help for Alibaba marketing and operations, while he got Joseph Tsai's help to bring in initial funding for the company. In 2005, Jerry Yang and Yahoo bet on Alibaba with a $ 1 billion investment. Years later, Yang assisted Ma in Alibaba's investment in messaging app Tango. Jack Ma never fails to acknowledge many people from his friends to his teammates for his success. And he is all the more a stronger leader and team player because of his gratitude and humility.

"No matter how smart you are, if you don't know how to work with people, your dreams will just be dreams." – Jack Ma

CHAPTER 5:

REMEMBER THAT "H" MATTERS

LESSON 13: BE HONEST

"We would rather close down the company than operate without integrity." – Jack Ma

More often than not, honesty as a virtue is often taken for granted, because it is perceived to be quite a basic one. However, overlooking integrity and honesty has far-reaching impacts as evidenced by the different scandals that have rocked government and business in the last decades.

Jack Ma: The Art of Dreaming &
Succeeding Extraordinarily

What does integrity really mean? It is doing the right thing even when it is difficult to do so. It is letting the truth be articulated even if it is difficult to hear. It means keeping your promises even if your circumstances have changed.

According to the late author, Douglas Adams, "To give real service you must add something which cannot be bought or measured with money, and that is sincerity and integrity." In both business and in life in general, honesty is a cornerstone in building trust. Trust, in turn, is the foundation of all kinds of relationships, including business.

Jack Ma places such high value on integrity that this is considered as one of Alibaba's core values. This was decided not during their pinnacle of success, but early on in Alibaba's journey. In 2002, at the time that it was so critical for Alibaba to start making profit, they made a firm stand of refusing to pay bribes even if that would have helped bring clients on board.

CHAPTER 5: REMEMBER THAT "H" MATTERS

As it turns out, even with this direction, two of Alibaba's best performers had resorted to paying off clients. Since these two accounted for about 60% of the company's sales, Jack was faced with the difficult decision as to whether to keep or dismiss them. He stayed true to their promised values, and finally let them go. He explained, "If we fire them immediately, the company will not have profit. If we do not kick these employees out, then what does this signify about us? It would imply that our words are empty."

The task of keeping their integrity has not been without difficulties, with occasional challenges coming along the way. In 2011, another scandal broke out when Ma admitted that some of their salespersons had accepted fraudulent sellers, and even accredited them as Gold suppliers, who never delivered their products. Again, Ma had to make the difficult choice of firing 100 employees, and being transparent about this incident.

To this day, Alibaba continues to walk the talk by having this principle ingrained in their company policies. According to Ma, "Our employees are not allowed to accept free car rides or meals. Small gifts, even a piece of candy, are sent back. If not, the employee's value score will be very low, and he or she could even be subject to penalties." To prevent bribery, the system is also supported by a clause written in client contract that states "Thank you for doing business with us. We hope that in our future business interactions, our employees cannot ask for bribes and you will not offer us bribes. If we discover any such situation, our group will never do business with you."

Ma likewise believes the value of transparency in doing business. At a certain point, Alibaba started charging its clients with annual fees. However, their clients were not immediately profitable, and revenues did not necessarily offset the fees. Rather than hiding details from their customers, the Alibaba sales team apologetically explained the pace of returns and gave them the opportunity to claim refunds. This transparency benefited the company by letting them earn their customers' trust for the long haul.

Aside from transparency, Ma places high importance on truth in sales training and advertising. Another Alibaba anecdote relates how Jack became upset with a trainer that was developing ways to pitch combs to monks who clearly did not need them.

As an E-Commerce enabler, Alibaba deals with a wide gamut of vendors and enterprises. As such, they have to deal with the issue of counterfeit products on a daily basis. While Ma acknowledges that the existence of fake products cannot be fully eradicated, he recognizes that presence of counterfeit goods hurts retailers and end-users. Vendors who advertise on Alibaba run the risk of having fellow suppliers copy their products, and they place their trust in company to provide sufficient protection for them. News reports that China harbors a $285 counterfeiting industry. Ma is rallying the government to improve its legal system to fight this, while Alibaba continues to lead the way in fighting counterfeit goods and intellectual property piracy.

In many interviews, Jack Ma repeatedly emphasizes the value of integrity and honesty in business. The question now is, can these be virtues be learned and how? There's a school of thought that espouses that these values are formed during childhood, and that they are difficult to learn after. However, many also subscribe to the idea that it is indeed possible to create an environment that supports integrity.

Here are some suggestions to consider. First, you can find an accountability partner. You can have a family member or friend hold you to your promises. You can also seek to be in an environment that encourages you to be better. Being surrounded by good influences can inspire you to increase your sense of integrity. Another idea is to find ways to keep yourself and your systems organized. Sometimes, failure to deliver on promises is not always a matter of deliberate choice, but maybe a case of a disorganized desk or missing checklist. While these ideas may be seemingly simple, they certainly are good first steps towards learning to lead yourself, and your team with more integrity.

"I find that when a person makes a mistake or fails, if he or she always complains or blames others, that person will never come back from the failure. But if the person checks inside, this person has hope." – Jack Ma

LESSON 14: BE HUMBLE

"Don't change because other people see you differently. Don't change because there's money in your pocket. Because there's one thing that can never change: your dreams, your values and your promises." – Jack Ma

The numbers and figures associated with Jack Ma's wealth are undoubtedly amazing to say the least. The richest man in China, his net worth is estimated to be at approximately $ 37 billion. His business Alibaba transacts more than the volume of Amazon and eBay combined. With his success and net worth, one would think that he would be a very proud man. The opposite however is true.

Currently, Ma owns only a little over 7% stake in Alibaba. While he remains Chairman of the conglomerate, he stepped down as CEO 4 years ago, with Jonathan Lu coming in to replace him. With his grand vision for Alibaba's global growth, he humbly recognized that he needed a better expert to steer the company in this direction. The move he says is also a step towards returning to his first love, teaching.

Jack Ma is indeed lauded by those who surround him as a very humble and down-to-earth leader. Oftentimes, people mistakenly associate humility with meekness or lack of confidence, and they therefore perceive this to be a weakness. This shouldn't be the case. Humility in leadership means being secure enough in one's self, so that there is awareness and acceptance of one's areas for improvement. Jack is always quick to acknowledge that he is not a technology or entrepreneurship guru. He in fact has always subscribed to the idea of bringing people who are more skilled than him into the team. Perhaps it can also be said that his humble background and his many experiences of rejection have grounded him into a leader who has largely remained simple and unassuming. Jack Ma has never let success get to his head. In fact, rather than rest on his laurels, he says "I am working harder than I ever did."

Prior to Alibaba's unprecedented IPO, Ma wrote a letter an email about it to his employees. In it, he had repeatedly expressed gratitude for their support, and gratitude for the privilege of the Internet, which they have used to succeed. He reminded them of the importance of remaining dedicated to work, and staying focused on helping small businesses, the primary reason for Alibaba's existence. Unlike announcements from other companies experiencing a similar milestone, Ma's letter consistently voiced his undeniable humility.

Why do we need leaders who are humble? Leaders who are humble are often easier to approach and work with. Simply put, they are easier to follow. Relatable heads are able to engage their teams better, making for more effective organizations.

CHAPTER 5: REMEMBER THAT "H" MATTERS

Leaders who are humble understand that their way of thinking and doing may not necessarily be always the most appropriate in all situations. This allows them to be more receptive to both feedback and change, making them more agile. Leaders who are humble are always willing to learn and improve themselves.

If you listen to Jack Ma's interviews, you will often hear about his desire to help small businesses and his countrymen. Service is at the heart of Jack's and Alibaba's vision. And if you think about it, this is what makes him an authentic leader, as leadership is all about one's willingness to serve. The principle of servant leadership espouses the importance of leaders both guiding and serving their organizations.

It will do leaders well to learn how to take a humble approach. There are different ways to go about it. Here are a few of them.

- **Gratitude** – Always keep a spirit of gratitude for the people around you. Remembering that any success you may reach is not solely attributable to yourself alone will allow you to remain humble. Aside from being mindful about giving thanks, it is likewise important to give credit where it is due. Not only will this ground you, it will also remind your team that their contributions are valued. Choose to engage your colleagues so that you can bring out the best in them, and not just the other way around.

- **Openness to Others' Ideas** – Always be willing to listen to others' ideas, even if they aren't necessarily the same as your line of thinking or even if they may sometimes sound weird. In a lot of ways, listening is hinged on acknowledging that you may not know everything, which is exactly what humility is all about. Be curious about what you don't understand. This will also help you foster more open listening.

And if you want to do as Jack Ma did, help yourself and your team embrace the spirit of service. With it, you will find just like Jack did, that selflessness allows you to give more, opening your way to success.

"I try to stay away from power, money and glory. If you keep power in your office, you will be in trouble. If you keep money in your own pocket, you will be in trouble. If you put glory on your head, you will be in trouble.... When you have money, spend it and support other people. When you have power, use it to empower others. And glory... give it to others." -- Jack Ma

LESSON 15: BE HUMAN

"Sooner or later, you will regret it if you spend all your time at work." – Jack Ma

Another misconception people have about successful and wealthy moguls is that all of them had to be cunning and ruthless to get to the top. Yes, there are many CEOs and heads who have gained notoriety for their unscrupulous and scheming practices. There are also seemingly heartless slave drivers who are focused solely on results and almost never on the soft side. However, it will also appear that most of leaders who have really reached the top, are actually kind, benevolent, and very human. Take the case of Bill Gates. For over 24 years, he has been in Forbes' list of top 400 richest Americans. At the same time, he and his wife Melinda are cofounders and chairs of the Bill & Melinda Gates Foundation, which happens to be the world's largest private charitable foundation. Mark Zuckerberg, founder of

CHAPTER 5: REMEMBER THAT "H" MATTERS

Facebook, has been known to have given hundreds of millions to help further education and public health.

And it need not be on the idea of charity alone. New schools of thought are now espousing the mindfulness and the ability to connect to a more human side as a leadership skill, that has now become all the more important at the workplace.

Leadership is more than ordering around people and telling them what to do. True leadership goes beyond getting results. It means influencing people towards a common goal by showing them how their personal goals can be achieved in the process. It means having an organization that believes that their leaders are personally invested in them as they are the company's objectives.

How can leadership be more humane?

People are looking to find meaning in their lives. It is important for an organization to have a vision worth buying into. The pioneering Alibaba team equally believed that their work contributed to a greater cause, that of helping China, by opening it up to the rest of the world. They believed that their work impacted the lives of many small enterprises in the country, making their work meaningful. In fact, they bought into their vision so much that even if the business was flailing in its initial years, they stuck with Alibaba.

Jack Ma also emphasizes the need to have more than just high IQ and EQ. Intelligence and knowing how to deal with people are important, but he explains that there is also such a thing as LQ or "the quotient of love, which machines never have". He says, "A machine does not have a heart, [a] machine does not have soul, and [a] machine does not have a belief. Human being have the souls, have the belief, have the value; we are creative, we are showing that we can control the machines." He believes that it is important for leaders to show compassion and kindness, as it is also the only way to get true respect.

Ma has shown us that it is possible to show love by this definition in a professional, corporate setting. Firstly, his team believes that he sincerely wants them to do better than him. This is consistent with his mantra of hiring people who he sees has potential. Jack has also repeatedly spoken about how in Alibaba, employee welfare is prioritized next to customers, and prioritized over shareholders. He says, "Next come our employees, because in today's knowledge economy, employees are most important in having satisfied customers. Without talented, happy, diligent and passionately committed employees, our commitment to serving customers will be empty. A company that does not have satisfied employees will not have satisfied customers, and without satisfied customers, we could not possibly have satisfied shareholders." One concrete example is how during Alibaba's IPO, stock grants to employees amounted to

as much as $250,000 per employee,
incentivizing them of course to stay with
the company.

Another characteristic of authentic
leadership is humility – a leader's ability
to openly accept criticism, and
acknowledge mistakes. Jack Ma humbly
admits that one of his biggest mistakes
was when he initially told his founding
partners that they could only go as far as
becoming managers in Alibaba since his
original plan was to hire experts from the
outside. He realized later on how big a
mistake that was and has since corrected
that by allowing these loyal partners to
take key positions in the conglomerate.

Finally, being more human means
recognizing that there is a time and place
for rest. Jack actually believes that rest
and relaxation are necessary breaks to
prepare one's self for the next sprint, be it
a short or long one. For him, success
also means being equally able to enjoy
life while working hard since "if you are

spending your whole life working, you will certainly regret it."

"There is strength in being human." – Jack Ma

CHAPTER 6:

ENJOY THE RIDE

LESSON 16: BE BOTH INSPIRED AND INSPIRING

Go big or go home. Otherwise, you are wasting your youth." – Jack Ma

To many, leadership may seem like a grand experience, echoed by pomp and circumstance. From an outsider's perspective, presidents and CEOs command attention and lead lives filled with perks. The truth however is, leadership on a day-to-day basis, isn't always so glamourous. Leaders have the daunting task of both self-leadership, and leading the teams that rely on them.

For an organization to do great things, good leaders don't just necessarily tell people what to do, they actually are the first doers, setting the bar for their teams. They inspire others by their example.

Real leaders show up consistently, day in, day out. Staying this focused is certainly not an easy task. Just like anybody else, they also have their bad days when they don't feel like doing this. Nonetheless, the mark of leadership is the ability to motivate one's self regardless of current personal circumstances.

As one of the world's most influential leaders, how does Jack Ma keep himself inspired so that he can continue inspiring others?

- **A Greater Purpose** - "We aim to build the future infrastructure of commerce. We envision that our customers will meet, work and live at Alibaba, and that we will be a company that lasts at least 102 years." This is Alibaba's vision, according to their website. You will notice that their vision doesn't really talk about money or profit. Alibaba seeks to be a cornerstone of commerce in order to change lives. Jack Ma's dream of helping small businesses all over the world is what keeps driving him forward, in both victorious and difficult times. His vision is strong enough to have kept him going even when Alibaba still wasn't profitable. It is also big enough to keep him excited for tomorrow even if it seems like the company has already reached the pinnacle of success.

- **The Goldilocks Rule in Goal-setting** – On an operational level, a goal that's too much of a stretch will likely overwhelm a person. The reverse of it, a goal which is too easy, fails to challenge and excite. In setting goals, it's best to remember the story of Goldilocks and the Three Bears. Just like how Goldilocks tested the beds and the chairs in the fairytale, you should be setting goals which are not too hard, not too easy, but just right. Jack Ma espouses this, and has been quoted many times to encourage people to take baby steps as necessary in achieving their goals.

- **Staying Curious** – Many achievements in Jack Ma's life have been spurred by his spirit of learning and curiosity – from how he learned English, to how he built a global empire. In fact, the story of Alibaba all started with a curious search for beer and China over the internet. It is this same spirit of continually asking and learning is what makes him one of the business world's biggest innovators. Likewise, this is the same spirit that keeps him refreshed and inspired. According to Ma, in this day and age where there is increasing possibility of artificial intelligence replacing standardized and predictable jobs, it is all the more important to teach the youth curiosity, creativity, and empathy, to allow them to keep up with the times.

- **A Dash of Fun** - Ma once said, "When I am myself, I am happy and have a good result." This is perhaps why even if others may have found him to be quite odd, Jack has always ingrained a fun-loving environment in Alibaba. While he and his team have been known to work very hard, they also take their play and recreation very seriously.

Jack Ma certainly has been one of modern China's most influential and inspiring leaders. Perhaps, author Orrin Woodward's quote captures his influence best - "Average leaders raise the bar on themselves; good leaders raise the bar for others; great leaders inspire others to raise their own bar."

"Trading is not about trading products. Trading is about the culture, passion, innovation and creation." - Jack Ma

LESSON 17: BE THE FUN

"I'm coming to this world not to work. I want to come to this world to enjoy my life. I don't want to die in my office. I want to die on the beaches." – Jack Ma

Did you know that there's such a thing as National Fun at Work Day? Indeed, there is! And it's supposedly celebrated every 28th of January.

Why have fun at work? The late American professor, Randy Pausch, once said, "Never, ever underestimate the importance of having fun." And in case you may not agree with the proverbial wisdom of the statement, "All work and no play makes Jack a dull boy," you may want to look up how Jack Ma runs Alibaba.

While Ma has built Alibaba with his team brick by brick with blood, sweat and tears, he is serious about not taking himself seriously all the time. It is not uncommon to see him singing karaoke or celebrating with his team at the office. It took years before Alibaba made a profit, so when they reached this milestone, Jack gave everyone a can of Silly String to play with. His quirky practices have included the secret operative that developed Taobao to do handstands during their breaks to keep them perked up!

A performer at heart, Jack has also been known to surprise his employees with song and dance numbers during company celebrations. Definitely not the average boss, Jack Ma rocked a nose ring and a Mohican wig to sing his employees Elton John's Can You Feel the Love Tonight at their annual party. During Alibaba's 18th year anniversary, he surprised the crowd by entering the stage, masked and on a motorcycle, and together with other executives, he channeled Michael Jackson in some dance moves! Alibaba's annual talent shows have become so ingrained in their culture that employees themselves take weeks to prepare their own performances.

While others may find his outlandish behavior weird, his fun-loving and charming demeanor has definitely won the hearts of his employees, who round up at every opportunity to take photos with him. Beyond just having fun, his team is loyal to him because they believe in the sincerity of his intentions towards his employees. He has become their mentor, their inspiration and father figure, all rolled into one, and in the same token, Alibaba has become family to him.

More than a just being a culture fun, Alibaba's corporate culture promotes inclusion and employee participation. How did this come about?

Although Ma's leadership style has been different and adapting depending on the circumstances of the business, he has been observed to also follow Management by Wandering Around, a style wherein managers go around their teams in an unstructured manner to check on and touchbase with them. As opposed to more formal meetings, this relaxed style allows subordinates to open up more easily about themselves and the daily happenings at work.

Aside from Ma's and executives' random visits, transparency is also encouraged with the use of "Aliway", their internal communications tool. Employees use Aliway as a venue to air their complaints and suggestions about problematic products, with the product development teams on hand to engage them in discussion. They likewise use this as a channel to address concerns even related to their job evaluations to get peer feedback on their performance.

Even though the company has grown exponentially from 18 to tens of thousands, the Alibaba organizational structure remains flat, which allows subordinates feel that they have access to their hierarchies. All employees, even the top executives, are asked to come up with nicknames for themselves when they join the company. Everyone is then encouraged to use these nicknames in addressing each other, again helping create a more open environment. Ma is Feng Qing Yang or "The Wind Blows Brisk and Light" while current CEO Daniel Zhang is Xiao Yao Zi or "free and unfettered man".

Alibaba employees, called internally as Aliren, also have a strong sense of family unity largely because of corporate activities which foster this. It is not uncommon for Ma to call for fun retreats for thousands of employees to get together. After Alibaba applied for its IPO, they also held a mass wedding for 102 employees to represent the 102 years that Ma projected for Alibaba's life. "The length of our marriage is 102 years, and we have 87 years left. After 87 years you can marry some else. But within these 87 years, you cannot change your mind," Ma, clad in traditional garments, toasted the couples.

Jack Ma: The Art of Dreaming &
Succeeding Extraordinarily

Held every 10th of May, Ali-Day is an annual festival meant to celebrate employees and to thank their families for their support. They started the celebration in commemoration of Alibaba's headstrong will to continue to operate even if the SARS epidemic in China in 2003 forced employees to stay at home.

Another important component of their culture is the Ali Ten Groups which seeks to promote camaraderie and inter-group communication. Now with over 10,000 members, the 42 clubs represent various hobbies and interests, including sports, arts, martial arts and Chinese traditional culture.

If there's anything that can be gleaned from these stories about Ma and Alibaba, it's that promoting a culture that promoting a culture that encourages fun and employee well-being certainly goes a long way in helping create brand success.

"Many painters learn by having fun, many athletes learn by having fun, many works [of art and literature] are the products of having fun. So, our entrepreneurs need to learn how to have fun, too." – Jack Ma

LESSON 18: BE A LITTLE CRAZY

"They called me crazy Jack. I think crazy is good. We are crazy, but we aren't stupid." – Jack Ma

Normally, when HR practitioners or headhunters profile executive positions, they look for certain factors in a person's history – educational background, the existence of an MBA degree, previous work experiences. It's as if a certain mold could predict success. However, if you think about it, the biggest industry gamechangers such as Steve Jobs, Bill Gates, Elon Musk and Jack Ma, would have broken the mold if there ever was one. They have certainly been different than the usual CEO, and if you were bold enough to say it, even a tad crazy.

But why are they so very successful if they aren't part of the usual suspects? Perhaps the copy of one of Apple's 1997 Think Different campaign ads can explain:

CHAPTER 6: ENJOY THE RIDE

"Here's to the crazy ones. The rebels. The troublemakers. The ones who see things differently. While some may see them as the crazy ones, we see genius. Because the people who are crazy enough to think they can change the world, are the ones who do."

People have always said that success requires a solid vision, a well-thought-out plan and effective implementation. Some would posit however that the missing ingredient is a dash of craziness, and perhaps, Jack Ma is the best example of this.

Jack Ma was crazy enough to be driven by passion instead of profit. He held on tightly to his visions for the company even if the early years were rough, and even if it took a while to get client and investor support.

He was crazy enough to think largely outside the confines of any box. It was certainly one thing to create new platforms for business like Alibaba or

TMall, but he went beyond that to dream up a complete ecosystem which included even payments and financing. He cast his vision not just for Chinese entrepreneurs and consumers, but made it one for the rest of the world.

He was crazy enough to be willing to lose face and fail repeatedly. He was even crazier to take every "No" as a challenge. From early education, to job-hunting, and on to business, for every rejection, he dusted himself and got back up every time.

He was crazy enough not to care about what others thought. While it probably hurt a bit to have been called "Crazy Jack", he laughed it off. While it probably felt bad to have his business model or his lack of tech background criticized, he shrugged it off. Naysayers used to say that Alipay wouldn't work. These days, there are about 520 million users who would say otherwise.

CHAPTER 6: ENJOY THE RIDE

Jack Ma was crazy enough to gamble big on Alibaba. And it paid off a million times over, not just for him and his team, but for China's economy as well.

Actor Will Smith once said, "Being realistic is the most common road to mediocrity. Why would you be realistic? What's the point? It just puts up a barrier."

Over the last few years, Ma and Alibaba have become China's definitive antithesis for mediocrity. And they are not slowing down any time soon. A performer at heart, Ma is now trying his hand at acting with a new martial arts film, Gong Shou Dao (The Art of Attack and Defence), with action stars Jet Li and Donnie Yen, to promote Tai Chi. And now, the soundtrack to the movie includes a duet Ma recorded with Chinese pop singer, Faye Wong!

Indeed, with Jack Ma and Alibaba, a little bit crazy is perfectly normal.

**"I hope to stay crazy for the next 30
years." – Jack Ma**

CONCLUSION

For Alibaba, what started as a vision for a marketplace which could connect businesses has become a full-fledged ecosystem. More than a decade ago, it would have been difficult to imagine a Chinese company being at par with Western businesses in terms of size and revenues. All these perceptions have now changed because of Alibaba.

Financial journalist Rebecca Fannin ascribes Alibaba's edge in the digital economy with the scope and scale of its businesses. "Alibaba is a combination of eBay (TaoBao), PayPal (AliPay), Amazon (TMall, Aliyun), Orbitz (Taobao Travel) and Google Play (Aliyun App Store) -- and of course, there's that Yahoo connection too... Plus, Alibaba has recently made several acquisitions that put the company into the hottest tech arenas: YouTube (Youku), Google mobile (Quixey and Shin Ma), Twitter (Weibo), Google Maps (AutoNavi) and WhatsApp (Laiwang, Tango)." Just like in a good game of chess, Ma had the foresight to position his businesses and align them towards where the global economies will be moving towards.

While Fannin pegs Ma as the Steve Jobs of China, with his "Jobs-like star quality, strategic vision and flair for promotion," this does not mean that success is suited only for people with similar qualities. If anything at all, the mercurial rise of the Alibaba group is proof that the formulas to success are not necessarily kept in secret, and in fact, can be learned by anyone.

This book sought to show principles of success as applied by Jack Ma and Alibaba, and a few suggestions on how these ideas could be practiced in daily living. While some readers may find a lot of the themes were similar or repetitive, this only goes to show that a lot of these values are actually related to one another, and that growing in one aspect can mean the need to strengthen in another area as well. The bite-sized suggestions were meant not to oversimplify the process of improving one's self, but to show that, in time and with patience, personal improvement can be gained. This book is by no means a complete literature for learning success. It is actually only an initial step in learning how to dream and how to reach for goals, as seen in Jack Ma's life. Readers are encouraged to take the step further and learn more, possibly through other materials, and of course, in actual practice, as this is what making things happen is really all about.

On Alibaba's first trading day in 2014 in the New York Stock Exchange, Jack Ma sat down with CNBC's "Squawk on the Street" anchors. He had with him a company souvenir shirt for the IPO. On the front was written, "Everyone should have a dream". The back said, "What if it is realized?". Years later, this message still rings true. Jack Ma dared to dream, believed in himself, and found a way to make it happen.

And the good news is, you can too.

Printed in Great Britain
by Amazon